Isobel

Mira

GW01367529

Errol

Illustrations © Sarah Pooley 1989
Text © Audrey Chappell 1989
First published 1989 by Blackie & Son Ltd

British Library Cataloguing in Publication Data

Pooley, Sarah
    A surprise for Oliver.
    I. Title
    823'.914[J]

    ISBN 0-216-92649-1

Blackie and Son Ltd
7 Leicester Place
London WC2H 7BP

Printed in Portugal

A Surprise for Oliver

Sarah Pooley and Audrey Chappell

Blackie

Every afternoon, Oliver went to nursery
school with his friends Sam and James.

He always took his friend Octopus with him.

Sometimes he wore Octopus round his neck
while he was painting.

He cuddled Octopus while he watched
television and drank his milk.

Sometimes he let his teacher wear Octopus
while he had a ride on one of the bikes outside.

One day Oliver helped to make a castle
with the big bricks.

When Mum came to collect him, Oliver
couldn't find Octopus anywhere.

Oliver's face grew very sad and wobbly.

At tea-time, Oliver just sat and sucked
his thumb.

The next day, when Oliver arrived at the
nursery, his teacher had a big smile on her face.

'I've got a surprise for everyone,' she said.

She took all the children into the
playground and ... there was Octopus!

He looked cosy and snug and quite
content with his new friend Shane.

Everyone was very pleased to see him ...
especially Oliver.

Batwoman
Jo

Kathy

Nicholas